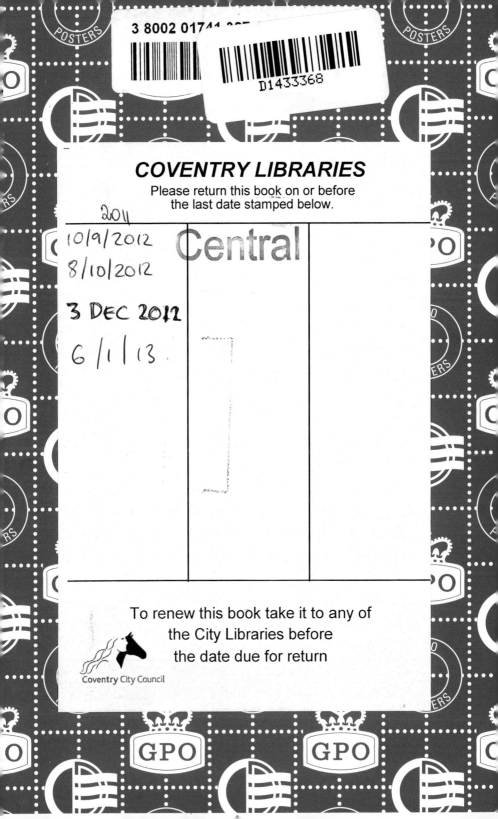

Paul Rennie

GPO
DESIGN
Posters

Antique Collectors' Club

Design Series format by Brian Webb

Design: GPO © 2011 Paul Rennie

ISBN 978-1-85149-596-2

British Library Cataloguing-in-Publication Data
A catalogue record for this book is available from the British Library.

Antique Collectors' Club
www.antiquecollectorsclub.com

Sandy Lane, Old Martlesham
Woodbridge, Suffolk IP12 4SD, UK
Tel: 01394 389950 Fax: 01394 389999
Email: info@antique-acc.com
or
ACC Distribution
6 West 18th Street, Suite 4B
New York, NY 10011, USA
Tel: 212 645 1111 Fax: 212 989 3205
Email: sales@antiquecc.com

Published in England by the Antique Collectors' Club Ltd.,
Woodbridge, Suffolk
Printed and bound in the United Kingdom

Pat Keely *Post Early in the Day* 1937, 253 × 380 mm, PRD 0173

Barry Wilkinson *Don't Spoil Your Holiday by Accident* 1964,
510 × 725 mm, IRP 195

Accident Prevention
The Post Office was a pioneer, during the 1940s and 1950s, of
promoting safe and efficient working practices. Many accidents
were the product of well-intentioned haste. The large
machines and speed required to process large volumes of
mail increased the risk of injury.

Preface

The status of posters as historical artefacts is increasingly acknowledged and the posters produced by London Transport, Shell Oil and the various railway companies are recognised as beautiful and significant documents of social history. Post Office posters, oft neglected, fully deserve to be recognised as part of this national achievement.

During the course of the 20th century, the Post Office successfully re-invented itself. Each of these re-inventions, whether prompted by political, social or technological factors, also required that the Post Office communicate those changes to its public. Under the terms of normal operations, the Post Office's public effectively comprised the entire population of Britain and, for much of the 20th century, its Empire, Dominions and Commonwealth. This placed the organisation at the forefront of public relations and global communication.

The material featured in this book was part of the attempt by the Post Office to make its services more widely understood. The posters presented here comprise three main types: educational posters for schools, posters providing information about services, and the more straightforward advertising material. Within each of these groups there are various themes that emerge. These themes speak of the men and women who provide the service, the communities they serve and the technology and organisational disciplines by which the services are assured. The Post Office organisation, its structure and its people are part of a culture of service that provides a powerful sense of collective identity. Understanding how organisations contribute to the collective identity is a crucial part of contemporary design practice; indeed, in order to be successful, design must be contextually appropriate.

H.A. Rothholz *Buy Stamps in Books* 1955, 507 × 755 mm, PRD 0799

Stamps in Books

The Post Office encouraged the purchase of stamps in books as a convenience to its customers. The reduction in number of the many thousands of small, stamp purchase type, transactions was a great help in reducing waiting time at its counters.

Design
GPO Posters

By 1918, the poster had become established as a powerful means of communication. The modern poster, distinguished by its characteristics of scale, colour, and the integration of image and text, has its origins in mid-19th century Paris. There, colour lithography was combined with new display opportunities made possible by the wide vistas of Baron Hausmann's redevelopment. In addition, economic and sociological change combined to associate the concentration of population with the material surpluses of industrial production.

The poster was quickly recognised as a uniquely economic and practical means of addressing the markets of the new leisure class. The cultural and aesthetic development of the poster, advanced by artists, industrialists and cultural entrepreneurs, further established the poster as an expression of modern life.

By the 1920s, the poster had entered a golden age of maturity in design, execution and display. In Britain, the large railway companies, London Transport, Shell-Mex and BP Ltd each promoted their activities through poster advertising.

By 1914, the Post Office had grown so as to employ 250,000 people and to have an annual revenue of £32.6m. This placed it amongst the very largest concerns of the time. Indeed, until the grouping and consolidations of the railways, in 1923, the Post Office was the largest single employer in Britain.

The legacy of WWI transformed the management of Post Office activities and helped introduce new ideas of discipline and responsibility to the workplace. The war also accelerated the process of mechanisation throughout the service. The process of integrating motorised transport into the logistics of the postal service was derived from the military experience of WWI (though full operational mechanisation was only finally achieved in 1950).

In turn, the process of mechanical and administrative modernisation increased the capacity of the service. Larger loads could be moved by motor lorries and those loads could be moved more speedily. In logistical terms it became easier, with telephone and telegraph services co-ordinated, to accurately locate men, machines and post within the great system. The major consequence of WWI was a substantial increase in the mechanical capacity and administrative efficiency of the service.

Also, the end of WWI was marked by a period of economic crisis, from which the Post Office was not immune. A combination of inflation and economic recession greatly reduced the profit margins of the postal service and pushed the Post Office into deficit. Increasing efficiency and maximising the volumes of each service suddenly became a priority for its political masters, and it was in this context that the Post Office began to engage in public relations in order to promote its services.

However, the civil servants of the Post Office were, for various reasons, relatively slow in acknowledging the importance of public relations. In practical terms, they had no experience of that world. Indeed, the historic development of the Post Office had eschewed advertising and public relations as inappropriate for an organisation of its status.

The forces of economic pressure and organisational inertia within the Post Office created peculiar and contradictory conditions. From 1921, the Post Office sold space within its public offices to other companies and organisations for commercial advertising. The revenue streams derived from this activity, whilst welcome, compromised the Post Office's own efforts at publicity. This conflict of interest was only resolved in 1935, when the commercial contracts were withdrawn.

Beyond the Post Office the antecedents of Government publicity were not auspicious. There were, for the administrators and managers of the Post Office, only two practical examples available: the poster propaganda of WWI and, later, that of the Empire Marketing Board (EMB), which had been established in 1926 with the objective of promoting trade relations between Britain and its Empire. Beyond the diplomatic efforts implicit in the EMB, the success of the project could only be assured by promotion to the largest possible audience. It made sense, in these circumstances, for the EMB to establish a Publicity Committee. Under the chairmanship of Sir Stephen Tallents, the Committee was charged with using the techniques of modern advertising to advance the arguments of the EMB.

The EMB produced, in total, some 800 posters. These were displayed in schools and on specially designed public display boards. The experience of the EMB convinced Tallents that Government publicity presented a more novel problem than commercial advertising. Paradoxically, noted Tallents, the use of communications made Government departments more accountable to the public and more open to criticism. He identified the main object of public relations as securing the co-operation of the public. Such co-operation was dependent, argued Tallents, on an understanding of the framework, or structure, of the practical and administrative efforts of the organisation.

In 1931 Ramsay MacDonald had appointed Clement Attlee as Postmaster General. Attlee was especially critical of the ambivalent promotion by the Post Office of its new telephone and airmail services. With this in mind, Attlee had spoken with Stephen Tallents at the EMB about how best to introduce modern advertising techniques and public relations within the organisation. Attlee quickly convened a Publicity Committee to advance the work of integrating public relations into the work of the Post Office. When the EMB was closed in 1933, Stephen Tallents moved to the GPO.

The success of the EMB encouraged Tallents to continue with a similar public relations strategy at the Post Office. Accordingly, his policy was to develop closer and more obvious links between the fine arts and the publicity material of the Post Office. To foster this effort, the Publicity Committee of the Post Office was strengthened by the addition of John Grierson and Jack Beddington. Beddington, like Pick at London Transport, was one of the major figures in British design reform during the 1930s. The Publicity Committee was supported by an Advisory Committee – including Kenneth Clark and the art critic Clive Bell – whose purpose was to identify suitable artists for consideration. The records show that Clark, Beddington and Tallents were in constant communication. Clark was behind the rationalisation of the scale of fees payable to artists for the use of their designs. He suggested that artists should be categorised, based on their professional reputations, as 'first class', 'established' and 'beginners'.

In 1935 Tallents left the GPO on his appointment as director of public relations at the BBC. Although his tenure at the Post Office had been relatively brief, Tallents had set in place systems that would serve the Post Office until well after WWII.

Maintaining the system was not, however, straightforward. Tallents was succeeded by Tristram Crutchley, who held an antagonism towards both modern art and collective decision-making. The origins and structures of the modern Post Office were shaped by the concern to standardise systems and service so as to eradicate fraud. Accordingly, the kinds of discursive and co-operative environments favoured by Tallents were not to his taste. Crutchley believed that artists and designers should simply be given a brief

A country Post Office in the 1930s

Vanessa Bell *The Last Minute* 1935, 635 × 509 mm (education format),
PRD 0112

ending of war credits. Accordingly, the specific circumstances of the post-war economy provoked an export-drive for foreign currency. Consequently, the usual activities of the advertising markets were greatly reduced and, as a result, many designers migrated to teaching. The Post Office was one of relatively few organisations that continued to provide a stable environment in which designers could work.

After 1951, the forces shaping British society shifted the focus of design away from the poster. In Post Office terms, this was most evident in the liberalisation of stamp design promoted from the early 1960s onwards and through the cultural phenomenon of collecting first day and commemorative covers. Much of the work in relation to design and cultural identity was accordingly transferred to the design and promotion of postage stamps.

Poster Themes: Education and Information

Tallents had taken, from his days at the EMB, a firm belief in the educational potential of poster design. In addition and specifically directed at Post Office customers, were posters providing information about new services and procedures.

A relatively small number of posters provided straightforward advertising messages about the Post Office. Aside from these three groups there were other posters relating to the safety and performance issues relating to the workforce. Across these variations, several themes emerged concerning the history, machinery, people and services of the organisation.

Educational posters were conceived to be displayed, on and off, for a number of years, and accordingly were on slightly thicker paper. The idea was that the poster images could be arranged to provide a changing pictorial display of trade, commerce, history and geography. The relatively static environment of school provided a different context for the display of images from those normally associated with advertising. These less dynamic environments required a more gentle type of image. Tallents, Beddington and Clark concurred that an artistic image, in broadly realist style, would be best suited to the job.

It is difficult, from our 21st century perspective, to imagine the relative austerity of most teaching environments before WWII. The opportunity to display pictures of any sort within a classroom setting had usually been confined to images drawn from biblical sources. Quite apart from any educational benefit, the school posters afforded the GPO a much-increased reach for their images. The school sets were printed in editions of about 30,000. Of these, only about 5,000 were displayed on Post Office premises. The school posters provide important evidence of the Post Office activities.

School sets of images were produced by the Post Office on this basis every year until 1939. The earliest commissions for these sets included HS Williamson's *Overseas Communications*, and John Armstrong's *History of Communications*. Armstrong and Williamson's posters provide, between them, eight images that span the history of communications and tell of the development of the GPO. Horsedrawn wagons, ships, aeroplanes at Croydon and a 1930s motorcycle courier supersede the fleet-footed messenger to the Ancients. Subsequent school posters include McKnight Kauffer's *Outposts of Britain*, John Vickery's *Outposts of Empire* and Eric Fraser's *Signals, Codes and Communications*. The Kauffer posters are unusual, within the context of pre-WWII poster design, for including photography within each design.

In addition to the educational posters the Post Office produced more straightforwardly commercial designs for information and advertising purposes. The campaign to *Post Early*, avidly promoted by Tallents, was first directed at easing the evening rush to catch the last postal collection of the day. This was soon extended to cover the busy period of post and parcels in the run-up to Christmas. In addition, as international communications and deliveries increased, the campaign was extended to apply to last postings for overseas delivery.

A number of posters ask that customers 'Please Pack Parcels Carefully'. Designers such as Tom Eckersley and Hans Unger produced these during the 1950s. These posters speak of an age where all kinds of oddly shaped things – such as salmon from Scotland or soft fruit – were manhandled through the postal system. They conveyed the convenience, economy and efficiency of standard packages. The increasingly standardised size, weight and volume of packages is a reflection of the, nowadays, widespread automation of the service.

The increasing volumes of service, made available through the combination of mechanisation and discipline, were expressed

Graham Sutherland *Post Early* 1934, 253 × 280 mm, PRD 0087

through the information graphics of Theyre Lee-Elliott, a pioneer of modernist information graphics and designer of the speedbird logo for Imperial Airways. The early efforts at pictographic information graphics were aimed at the presentation of statistics. This information was used to justify the plans of centralised command economies and their claims to progress. (These kinds of graphic presentation became increasingly unfashionable in the West during the Cold War.) The presentation of this kind of information was, by contemporary standards, technically limited. The expansion of Post Office machinery and services was an ideal subject for this kind of presentation.

More obviously related to commercial advertising were the posters produced to promote the convenience of the new telephone services and airmail routes. During and after WWII, the urgent and uncertain economic conditions provided the context for the sustained promotion of the Post Office Savings Bank.

The pictorial themes of Post Office posters remained remarkably consistent. The historical development of the service is presented as part of a consistent and continuous extension of the social good provided by the Royal Mail. Typically, the historical development of the Post Office is shown by reference to the vehicles associated with the mechanisation of the service – trains, boats and aeroplanes. However there is another theme, implicit within these images, that the organisation of the service is itself an elaborate mechanism and a reflection, or exemplification, of the clockwork of society.

Automation and mechanical organisation of society is now understood as a characteristic of modern society. In the 1930s, the workings and consequences of this organisation were much less obvious. The Machine Age of the inter-war years could be understood as either an expression of Utopian progress or as that of a dystopian and alienating system. The ambiguity and anxieties attaching to this kind of progress were captured, at the time, in Fritz Lang's *Metropolis* (1926) and Huxley's *Brave New World* (1932).

John Armstrong *The King's Messenger* 1935, 635 × 509 mm, PRD 0057

John Armstrong *Mail Coach 1784* 1935, 635 × 509 mm, PRD0104

Against a background of dystopian politics of the 1930s, the Post Office was able to provide a narrative of both technical and humane progress. The organisation of the Post Office is presented as both a socially constructed organisation and as a mechanical system or organisation.

The various phases of WWII created a series of new opportunities for poster design and graphic communication in Britain. In the early phase, a number of messages were created to address the civilians and workers whose contributions were part of the homefront. After 1941, a new type of communication began to express values that were part of the post-war agenda of social democratic reconstruction.

The extension of the Post Office campaign into schools and the consistent use of posters and cinema for the delivery of its public relations show the Post Office to have understood the economies of scale made possible by the new technologies of mass-communication. Indeed it is worth considering that, notwithstanding the avant-garde experimentation in Germany and the Soviet Union during the 1920s, the structures established by Tallents provide for the most successful, radical and consistent expression of Modernist design values.

Royal Mail motorcycle delivery 1930s

Loading the Airmails - Croydon 1930s

Technological Advancements

Printmaking and the processes of making images have, until relatively recently, been shrouded in mystery. The origins of the modern poster were made possible by the development of colour lithography. Quite apart from the mysteries of lithography – incidentally, a process of quite magical potential – the development of colour lithography required enormous resources. Each colour required a separate printing. So a six-colour design would require the printing of the edition six times over to achieve the complete and finished result.

Graphic design developed, in part at least, as a way of minimising the costs attached to printing these images. This was achieved by economies of design through simplification. It was precisely this simplification that began to distinguish Modernist design in the 1920s.

The simplification of design into the assembly of typographic and photographic elements was only part of the economic transformation of 20th century image culture. The mechanical reproduction of images, promoted by Walter Benjamin and others, was dependent on the new print technology of four-colour, offset litho. This process combined the production of different colours and effects into the overprinting of four colours. These were identified as CMYK: cyan, magenta, yellow and key (black). A print, comprising a vast range of colour effects could be produced by a single pass through the press.

Notwithstanding these technical developments, the economy of poster printing remained generally under-developed. The resources required to print poster-sized images using traditional colour lithography had tended to concentrate resources, both of skills and plant, into fewer and larger-scaled companies. The capacity, within this system, was able to respond to the commercial demands of

Pat Keely *Night Mail* (artwork) 1939, 700 × 544 mm

Robert Harling *Post in the Morning* 1941, 920 × 735 mm, PRD 0253

the 1930s quite easily. In this context, commercial inertia and political economy conspired to resist the introduction of new technology.

Although the rationing of paper during WWII resulted in far fewer commercial posters, there was a greatly increased demand for official poster communications and a greater urgency in their production. In practical terms, the advent of war compressed the technical evolution of the print industry into a very short period. The commercial pain usually associated with this kind of technical transformation was effectively camouflaged by the circumstances of war.

During the 1950s, a similar process of simplification was directed at the craft technologies of screen-printing. The mechanical make-ready of screens made short-run poster printing an economically viable activity. It is unsurprising that, in these circumstances, several designers (including Tom Eckersley, working at the London College of Printing) should experiment with the potential of screen-print.

The Artists & Designers

The Post Office was able, through its efforts in advertising, to offer employment to fine artists, commercial artists and graphic designers. It is fair to say that a large proportion of the artists and designers associated with the Post Office campaigns remain, even today, relatively obscure and that the role of poster designer remained a fragile economic activity throughout most of the 20th century.

When Stephen Tallents arrived at the GPO in 1933 from the Empire Marketing Board he brought a number of artist associates with him. The composition of the Committee brought additional influence and recommendation through Kenneth Clark and Jack Beddington.

One of the earliest artists to accept a commission from the GPO, and surely one of the best known, was Paul Nash in 1934; although, ultimately the commission would come to nothing. Through his position at the RCA, Nash had himself been at the forefront of recommending and promoting a generation of artists to Frank Pick at London Transport, Harold Curwen at the Curwen Press and to Jack Beddington at Shell. Positioning himself at the head of the English avant-garde, he established the group Unit One with Ben Nicholson in 1933, with the aim of promoting modern art, architecture and design in Britain, and to provide an environment in which artists, sculptors, architects and designers could meet. From this point in his career, the exact meanings of Nash's work became increasingly ambiguous; he was one of the first to incorporate surrealistic elements into commercial communication.

The relative ambiguity of Nash's images and the obscure meanings of his surrealistic imagery required courageous patronage and led to the Committee's decision that it was unable to find an appropriate use for Nash's submission.

Another member of Unit One, theatre designer and surrealist John Armstrong, had rather more success with the GPO. His group of four *Messengers* (1934) provided a pictorial history of the Royal Mail from the time of the ancients through to the 1930s. Having already produced a number of posters throughout the 1930s for Jack Beddington at Shell, Armstrong most likely received his commission through Beddington's association with the Advisory Committee. Similarly, Graham Sutherland's successful designs for Beddington at Shell probably prompted his commission for the *Post Early* campaign.

The Publicity Committee also awarded early commissions to Duncan Grant and Vanessa Bell – both members of the influential Bloomsbury set. The Bloomsbury artists had, since their collaboration with Roger Fry at the Omega Workshops, pursued the integration of art and life through design. The Bloomsbury project should probably be identified with the later stages of the 19th century Arts and Crafts movement. Accordingly, it should be understood as a retreat from social democratic forms of modernity rather than as part of a cultural engagement with a wider and more socially varied audience.

In 1934, Duncan Grant designed a set of four portraits in a social-realist style, which drew attention to the numbers of engineers and back-room staff. Interestingly, the titles of the images drew attention to the numbers of people employed in each capacity. From the current perspective of obsession with labour costs it is amazing to see an organization trumpeting the scale of its staff numbers. The kinds of portraits produced by Grant became a staple of home-front propaganda during WWII.

Also in 1934, Vanessa Bell produced an artistic design as part of the *Post Early* campaign in which last-minute customers besieged a Post Office counter clerk. The committee, however, judged the image inappropriate. The rejection of Bell's picture may well have played a part in setting off a critical discussion of the relative merits of Post Office advertising in relation to those of Shell.

Clive Bell began a critical campaign in which the artistic standards of Post Office advertising were called into question. The Post Office answered fine art critics through an article by John Cuff in *Penrose* (1939), who made the point that it was pointless to judge commercial work by Bloomsbury standards. The address of Post Office publicity material was necessarily much wider in scope than that of Shell, in an age when car ownership was still limited. Of course, since Clive Bell, Beddington and Tallents were all colleagues, the argument seems, with hindsight at least, a little incestuous. The advertising departments of both organisations, although unconnected, were guided by the personalities of Tallents and Beddington. In any event, the argument was soon overtaken by the events associated with the outbreak of WWII.

In the main, the most successful poster designs came from artists who were already working in the field of commercial art. These artists were already used to the issues of typography, lettering and communication. Commercial art, as an activity, was distinguished by the production of original artwork to a more or less finished standard. Print technicians and lithographic artists then interpreted the original by reproducing it as faithfully as possible.

Working in this tradition, McDonald Gill became a specialist in producing decorative maps of trading routes. Gill attached himself, as a designer, to organisations supporting Britain's imperial relations. Not surprisingly, he produced maps for the EMB (1927) and later for the Post Office (1934). These map diagrams were complex and included a wealth of cartographic information, decoration and typography.

The system of commercial art had evolved in relation to the technical demands of print management and to the expanding demands of the visual communications to support the political and economic organisation of society. By the 1930s, the system had just about grown to its limits. The cost, in time and resources, of

producing visual communications had placed this material beyond
all but the largest firms.

New economic methods of visual communications would depend,
in the future, on the increasing mechanisation, and automation, of
the production process. So, from the mid-1930s onwards, a new
type of work was to be seen. This involved a greater use of
photography and an embrace of mechanical reproduction. The role
of designer began to emerge, in relation to these technologies, as
one of technocratic specification and assembly rather than as
simple origination.

When in 1932 they were commissioned by the GPO, Austin
Cooper and Frank Newbould were already senior figures in
advertising and poster design, in particular having produced work
for the LNER (London and North Eastern Railway). LNER publicity
material was managed by William Teasdale, who quickly grasped
the importance of creating a consistent and uniform identity for
the new railway group, including the use of consistent typography
for all its communications. The LNER used Eric Gill's *Sans* face,
designed for Monotype, on everything from its posters through to
engine nameplates.

The Post Office engaged in a similar process of developing its
corporate identity through design and typographic coherence.
Though, on the basis of the posters shown here, it appears to have
done this less consistently than both London Transport and the LNER.

Cooper and Newbould brought a sense of light-heartedness,
derived from their jaunty seaside advertising for LNER, to the
design work of the Post Office. This feeling had been conspicuous
in its absence from the rather seriously educational work of the
artist designers. The sense of humour in their design was expressed
through the jaunty colour palette favoured by both Cooper and
Newbould. Cooper's own hand-rendered lettering also exploited
traditions of signage associated with public entertainments.

Airmail Services 1930s

H.S. Williamson *Loading Mails for the Empire – Croydon 1934* published 1936, 635 × 509 mm, PRD 0142

The single most important personality in design between the wars was Edward McKnight Kauffer. From 1916 onwards, Kauffer had begun to position himself as a commercial artist and designer. His early success with London Transport quickly assured his reputation, and by the 1930s Kauffer was able to add Shell and the Post Office to his extensive list of clients. Indeed, by the end of the decade, Kauffer was acknowledged as the senior figure within commercial design in Britain.

Kauffer made a number of contributions to the Post Office campaign including, in 1937, a famous set of *Outposts of Britain*. The four posters in this series show Kauffer attempting to frame photographic elements within an art context.

Inspired by Kauffer, a small group of younger designers began to emerge under the patronage of 1930s design reform. Pitting themselves against the established heavyweights of poster design and fighting for a place despite the exclusionary practice of concentrating resources amongst the big lithographic printers, Pat Keely, Tom Eckersley and Theyre Lee Elliott had each established their reputations by the outbreak of WWII.

Eckersley had a remarkable career in design comprising four distinct contributions. The first was a commercial artist designer with his colleague Eric Lombers. Later, Eckerlsey was able to combine his war work as a cartographer in the RAF with the design of posters for the Royal Society for the Prevention of Accidents. These posters pioneered the visual communication of safety propaganda. After the war, this kind of design became a powerful and important tool in the projection of values associated, throughout Europe, with post-war reconstruction. The post-war European connection was further developed through Eckersley's association, from early on, with Alliance Graphique (AGI). This body brought together the major protagonists of European graphic design. The resulting network facilitated the exchange of ideas and the development of an appropriate graphic style for the projection and communication of messages beyond the entirely commercial.

After 1945, a new type of communication began to express values that were part of the post-war agenda of social democratic reconstruction. Finding designers able to relate to these values and to produce images in which modernity and social democracy were aligned proved more difficult than anticipated. The older generation had become increasingly associated, through their professional CVs, with the discredited values of the 1930s. Younger, British designers were mostly attached to the various services and busy with their military duties. Luckily, a group of émigré designers had arrived in Britain during the 1930s and were able to contribute to this development.

The most important of these were FHK "Henri" Henrion and Hans "Zero" Schleger. Along with Abram Games and Tom Eckersley, these designers formed a group that effectively transformed British graphic design in the post-war period. Both Henrion and Schleger produced posters in the 1940s before becoming increasingly involved with the development of corporate identity and the integrated design of large-scale industrial, commercial and social organsiations.

In the short term, the design environment immediately after WWII was distinguished by a sharp contraction in spending in response to the economic costs of military success being actually far greater than had been expected. In addition, the specific circumstances of the post-war economy provoked an export-drive for foreign currency. Consequently, the usual activities of the advertising markets were greatly reduced. As a result, many of the designers who had been active during WWII migrated to teaching in the aftermath of the war. Apart from that, the Post Office was one of relatively few organisations that continued to provide a stable environment in which designers could work.

A number of émigré designers were able to work for the Post Office, including Arnold Rothholz, who had arrived in Britain at the end of the 1930s and would work with the Post Office for nearly 20 years; Hans Unger, whose graphic style that allowed for the integration of "pop" elements in the early 1960s; Jan Le Witt and George Him, in collaboration under the name Lewit-Him; and Manfred Reiss, who was awarded several commissions by the GPO during his career as a poster designer in Britain.

The émigré designers made a unique and substantial contribution to the development of graphic design in Britain. In terms of poster design, they were able to integrate a number of ideas that had originally been part of the European modernist surrealist movement. The use of montage techniques, beyond the simple process of assembling photographic elements, allowed for an increasing psychological space within graphic communication. This required a combination of skills based on modernist design formation and also an "outsider's" eye attuned to the quirky and to seeing things differently.

Post Office posters are part of the visual expression of ideas, through graphic design, that connect the disparate parts and activities of society into a coherent and systematic or coherent whole. The system combines elements that, from the philosophical Enlightenment and scientific revolution onwards, have come to exemplify modern life.

The posters, collected here, remind us that design is an activity that is simultaneously creative, practical and philosophical.

F.H.K. Henrion *Post Early* 1949, 253 × 380 mm, PRD0554

John Vickery *Outposts of Empire:*
Barbados, Central Australia, Southern Rhodesia, Ceylon
1937, each 635 × 509 mm, PRD 0184, 0185, 0186, 0187

OUTPOSTS OF EMPIRE   SOUTHERN RHODESIA

OUTPOSTS OF EMPIRE   CEYLON

Educational Prints

The Post Office was quick to acknowledge the importance of education in its public relations. Sets of four images were produced in royal format (25 × 20 in 635 × 509 mm) and printed on heavier paper stock. These images were printed in large editions and sent to schools to be displayed in classrooms. The educational benefits of a less austere visual environment were quickly acknowledged.

ROYAL MAIL. A.D. 1935

Previous spread: John Armstrong *Royal Mail 1935* (motorcycle messenger)
1935, 635 × 509 mm, PRD 0059

Jesse Collins *Postman in the Potteries* (artwork) 1955, 609 × 492 mm

H.S. Williamson *Mails for the Packets Arriving at Falmouth 1833* 1934,
635 × 509 mm, PRD 0095

H.S. Williamson *Loading Mails at the Dock in London 1934* 1934,
635 × 509 mm, PRD 0140

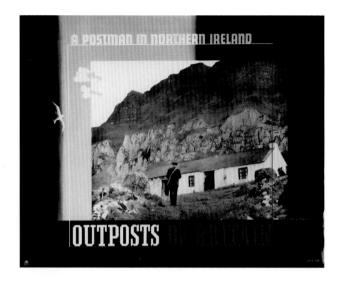

Edward McKnight Kauffer *Outposts of Britain:*
Northern Ireland, the Pool of London, Northern Scotland, Land's End
1937, each 635 × 509 mm, PRD 0163, 0164, 0165, 0166

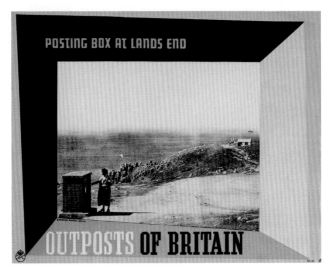

Framing Photography

Edward McKnight Kauffer's *Outposts of Britain* posters show clearly the various attempts made to frame photographic elements within an existing tradition of artistic lithography. The technical limits of mechanical reproduction were such that, during the 1930s, only a small part of the whole design could be derived from a photographic original. A solution was to group photo elements together, in montage. Alternatively, the photo elements could be framed within geometric windows. Here, Kauffer's frames provide three-dimensional emphasis to the images.

Micheal Ross *Sorting Machine at Mount Pleasant* (artwork) 1937, 712 × 586 mm

Grace Golden *A London Telegraph Messengers' Despatch Room* (artwork) 1948, 630 × 504 mm

G.R. Morris *The Post Office Handles 23,000,000 Letters a Day* (artwork)
1947, 670 × 539 mm

Donia Nachshen *The Other Side of the Counter* 1943, 920 × 735 mm, PRD 0312

F.H.K. Henrion *Post Office Lines of Communication* (artwork) 1947,
467 × 380 mm

Lewitt-Him (Jan Le Witt and George Him) *Post Office Lines of Communication*
(artwork) 1950, 675 × 540 mm

Hans Schleger (Zero) *Post Office Lines of Communication – Telegrams* (artwork)
1947, 452 × 355 mm

John Barker *Post Office Lines of Communication* (artwork) 1947, 515 × 463 mm

Eric Fraser *Post Office Savings Bank* (convoy supplies) 1943, 920 × 735 mm,
PRD 0286

Eric Fraser *Post Office Savings Bank* (factory production) 1942, 920 × 735 mm,
PRD 0274

Frank Newbould *Save for National Safety* 1939, 253 × 380 mm, PRD 0230

Savings and Exports
The Post Office Savings Bank played a crucial role in supporting the
industrial production of WWII. The rapid expansion of the industrial
base transformed the workplace and the types of work available,
especially for women workers. After the war, the Post Office promoted
its services in support of export markets.

Hans Schleger (Zero) *GPO Helps the Export Drive* 1948, 920 × 735 mm,
PRD 0576

Hans Schleger (Zero) *Think Ahead Write Instead* 1945, 920 × 735 mm,
PRD 0414

Edward McKnight Kauffer *Quickest Way by Air Mail* 1935, 505 × 755 mm,
PRD 0111

Air Mail
The advent of scheduled air travel during the 1920s and 1930s
allowed the Post Office to provide Air Mail deliveries around the
world. Many posters were produced to draw attention to the speed
and economy of this modern service.

M. H. Armengol *For Overseas Parcels It's Quicker by Air* 1953, 253 × 380 mm,
PRD 0704

Bruce Roberts *Send Your Overseas Parcels by Air Mail* 1951, 253 × 380 mm,
PRD 0624

Lewitt-Him (Jan Le Witt and George Him) *Airgraphs Get Priority* 1943,
1300 × 355 mm, PRD 0318

Pieter Huveneers *Send Your Overseas Parcels by Air Mail* 1954,
920 × 735 mm, PRD 0741

Austin Cooper *Send Airgraphs - They Save Aircraft Space* 1942,
1300 × 355 mm, PRD 0271

Ronald Watson *By Air Mail* (artwork) 1935, 550 × 760 mm

Bruce Roberts *Buy Stamps in Books They Save Time* 1950, 253 × 380 mm, PRD 0573

Donald Smith *Save Time Buy Stamps in Books* 1950, 253 × 380 mm, PRD 0585

Bruce Roberts *Save Time Buy Your Postage Stamps in Books* 1949,
253 × 380 mm, PRD 0518

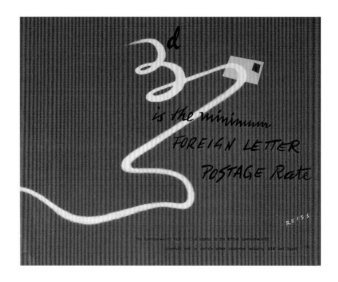

Manfred Reiss *3d is the Minimum Foreign Letter Rate* 1949,
920 × 735 mm, PRD 0548

Tom Eckersley *4d Minimum Foreign Rate* 1951, 920 × 753 mm, PRD 0620

Leonard Beaumont *4d is the Minimum Foreign Letter Postage Rate* 1952,
920 × 735 mm, PRD 0659

Bruce Roberts *4d Minimum Foreign Letter Postage Rate* 1956,
920 × 735 mm, PRD 0828

H. Blyth *Catch the Noon Post* 1942, 1070 × 265 mm, PRD 0276/2

H.A. Rothholz *Catch the Noon Post* 1942, 1300 × 355 mm, PRD 0275

Hans Schleger (Zero) *Post Before Lunch* 1941, 1070 × 265 mm, PRD 0251

Austin Cooper *Post Early and Don't Miss the Noon Post* 1942, 1300 × 355 mm,
PRD 0243/2

Strip posters

Strip posters are distinct to the Post Office. Displayed on the sides of delivery
vans and lorries, they provided a practical and economical way of
communicating with the public whilst out-and-about.

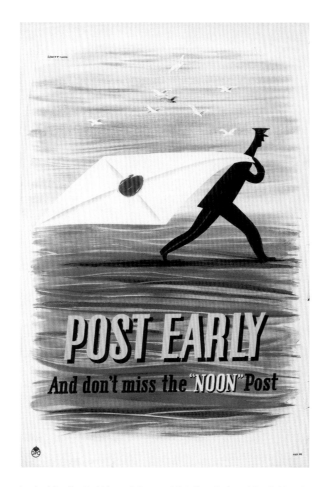

Lewitt-Him (Jan Le Witt and George Him) *Post Early and Don't Miss the Noon Post* 1941, 505 × 755 mm, PRD 0242

Leonard Beaumont *Nineteenth December – Finish Your Postings for Christmas*
1942, 1300 × 355 mm, PRD 0176/6

Hans Schleger (Zero) *Post Even Earlier this Christmas* 1944, 1300 × 355 mm,
PRD 0395

W. Machan *Post Early this Christmas* 1945, 1300 × 355 mm, PRD 0425

Eric Fraser *Post Early this Christmas* 1946, 1300 × 355 mm, PRD 0451

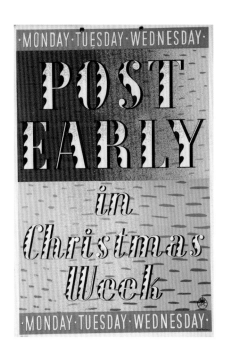

Barnett Freedman *Post Early this Christmas* 1938,
253 × 380 mm, PRD 0175/2

Barnett Freedman *Post Earlier for this Christmas*
1937, 253 × 380 mm, PRD 0175

Post Early

The tendency of many people to post letters at the last minute posed a very
big problem for the Post Office. The work of the Post Office was divided into
daytime collection, delivery and sorting and night-time transfer. The large
volumes of post, late in the day, made the allocation of resources and the
efficient provision of service much more complex and costly.
These images are part of the more or less continuous campaign to promote
discipline amongst the public in relation to the Post office service.

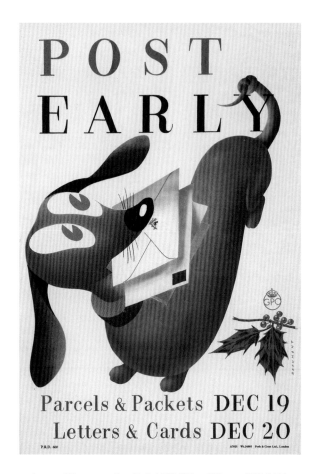

Leonard Beaumont *Post Early* 1950, 253 × 380 mm, PRD 0600

Tom Eckersley *Be First Not Last – Post Early* 1955 , 253 × 380 mm, PRD 356

Leonard Beaumont *Post Early Parcels and Letters* 1947, 253 × 380 mm, PRD 0498

Manfred Reiss *Travel Shop Post Early* c.1952, 253 × 380 mm, PRD 0690

H.A. Rothholz *Post Early* 1951, 253 × 380 mm, PRD 0647

Robert Scanlan *Post Early* 1961, 920 × 735 mm, PRD 1243

Hans Unger *Post Early* 1958, 920 × 735 mm, PRD 0988

Leonard Beaumont *Post Earlier than you did Last Year* 1943, 1300 × 355 mm,
PRD 0341

Lewitt-Him (Jan Le Witt and George Him) *Post Much Earlier this Year* 1941,
1300 × 355 mm, PRD 0176/4

Lewitt-Him (Jan Le Witt and George Him) *Post Early Again this Christmas* 1941,
1300 × 355 mm, PRD 0176/5

Eric Fraser *Post Early and Don't Miss the Noon Post* 1942, 1300 × 355 mm,
PRD 0243/2

Tom Eckersley *Address Your Letters Plainly* 1942, 1300 × 355 mm, PRD 0261/2

Barnett Freedman *Post Early this Christmas* 1937, 1300 × 355 mm, PRD 0176/2

Leonard Beaumont *Post Earlier for this Christmas* 1945, 1070 × 265 mm, PRD 177/3

Hans Schleger (Zero) *Address Your Letters Plainly* 1942, 1070 × 265 mm, PRD 0262

Lewitt-Him (Jan Le Witt and George Him) *Your Christmas Packets and Parcels Should be Posted by Dec 18th* 1941, 380 × 253 mm, PRD 0257

Edward McKnight Kauffer *Post During Lunch Hour* 1937,
253 × 380 mm, PRD 0156

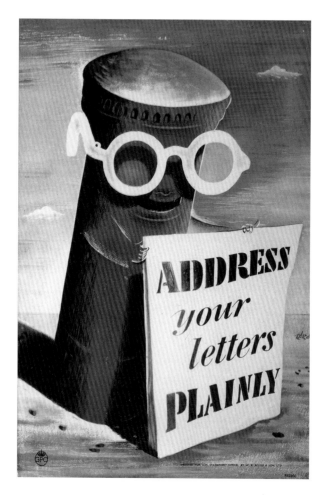

Hans Schleger (Zero) *Address Your Letters Plainly* 1942, 253 × 380 mm,
PRD 0260

Address Plainly

In its modern form, the postal service played a key role in encouraging
the standardisation of address information. House numbering, street
naming, postal districts and postcodes began to distinguish a new kind
of urban geography. The Post Office produced many posters
encouraging the public to adopt these standard forms as a way of
maximising economy and speed in the service.

Stan Krol *Use Block Letters for Telegrams* 1950, 253 × 380 mm, PRD 0563

Craig *Use Block letters for Telegrams* 1951, 253 × 380 mm, PRD 0619

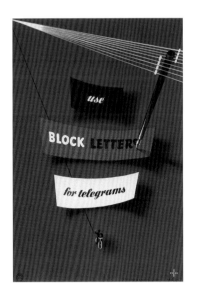

Hans Unger *Use Block Letters for Telegrams* 1951, 253 × 380 mm, PRD 0615

P. Vinten *Please Use Block Letters for Telegrams* 1947, 247 × 367 mm, PRD 0480

Leonard Beaumont *Before Sending Your Postal Order* 1955, 920 × 735 mm,
PRD 0773

Manfred Reiss *Address Your Letters Correctly* 1950, 253 × 380 mm, PRD 0575

R. Coombs *Address Your Letters Clearly and Correctly* 1950, 253 × 380 mm, PRD 0545

Tom Eckersley *Address Your Letters Correctly–And Clearly and Completely*
1944, 920 × 735 mm, PRD 0380

Leonard Beaumont *Address Your Mail Clearly and Correctly* 1956, 920 × 735 mm,
PRD 0857

Anon *Remember to Use Your Postal Code* 1967, 253 × 380 mm, PRD 1747

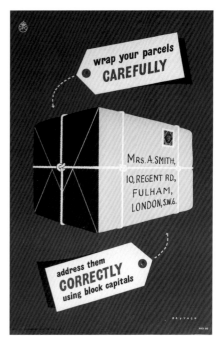

Hans Unger *Pack Your Parcels Carefully* 1949,
253 × 380 mm, PRD 0546

Dennis Beytagh *Wrap Your Parcels Carefully* 1952,
253 × 380 mm, PRD 0640

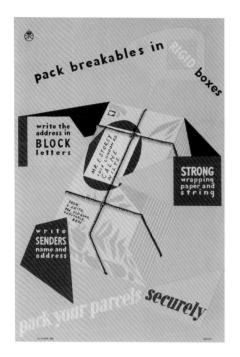

Anon *Pack Breakables in Rigid Boxes* 1950,
253 × 380 mm, PRD 0570

Caswell *Wrap Your Parcels Carefully* 1953,
253 × 380 mm, PRD 0696

Hans Unger *Pack Your Parcels Carefully* 1960, 920 × 735 mm, PRD 1094

Tom Eckersley *Please Pack Parcels Very Carefully* 1957, 920 × 735 mm,
PRD 0877

Dan Reisinger *Please Pack Your Parcels Carefully* 1959, 920 × 735 mm, PRD 1030

certain articles need special packing · ask at counter for free leaflet

George Brzezinski (Karo) *Properly Packed Parcels Please* 1968, 920 × 735 mm, PRD 1970

James Matutus Judd *Pack Your Parcels Carefully* 1962, 920 × 735 mm, PRD 1310

Tidal *Post Offices in the United Kingdom On Sale Here Invaluable in the Office* 1946, 253 × 380 mm, PRD 0446

Tom Eckersley *Post Office Guide Oct 1947* 1948, 253 × 380 mm, PRD 0458

Guides

The Post Office was always at the forefront of business information. From the first it collated directories of the businesses and services available in cities throughout Britain. These provided a valuable resource for marketing and sales departments. The directories were updated every year.

Lewitt-Him (Jan Le Witt and George Him)
A Postal Guide to the Maze of London 1951,
505 × 755 mm, PRD 0639

B. Orna *London Post Offices and Streets New Issue
March 1950* 1950, 253 × 380 mm, PRD217

Tom Eckersley *Buy the New Post Office Guide* 1949, 920 × 735 mm, PRD 0541

Pat Keely *A Guide To All Post Offices* 1945, 920 × 735 mm, PRD 0420

Alick Knight *On Sale Here – Post Office Guide* 1951, 920 × 753 mm, PRD 0631

Hans Unger *Guide To All Charges and Services - Post Office Guide* 1957,
253 × 380 mm, PRD 0883

Alick Knight *On Sale Now 2/6* 1961, 253 × 380 mm, PRD 1188

H.W. Browning *Cancel All Stamps. Stamps Missed – Revenue Lost* 1952,
510 × 760 mm, IRP 059

Peter Laufer *Inland Post Register Your Valuables* (artwork) 1953,
253 × 380 mm, PRD 0666

Acknowledgements

I acknowledge the kind help of the British Postal Museum and Archive in facilitating this project. I am especially grateful to Deborah Turton and colleagues for all their kind help.

Bibliography

Anthony S. (2007), *Night Mail*, London, BFI

Aulich J. (2007), *War Posters*, London, IWM and T&H

Aynsley J. (2000), *Graphic Design in Germany*, London, T&H

Barden M. (1993), *Post Early (GPO Posters)*, London, Camberwell

Barman C. (1979), *The Man Who Built London Transport*, Newton Abbot, D&C

Black M. (1956), 'Post Office Printing', *Penrose Annual*, Volume 50, p56, London, Lund Humphries

Bos B. & E. (2007), *AGI – Graphic Design Since 1950*, London, T&H

Bownes D. & Green O. (2008), *London Transport Posters*, London, LTM and LH

Constantine S. (1986), *Buy and Build (EMB posters)*, London, PRO

Cooper A. (1938), *Making a Poster*, London, Studio

Cuff J. (1939), 'Post Office Publicity', *Penrose Annual*, Volume 41, p22, London, Lund Humphries

Daunton M.J. (1985), *Royal Mail*, London, Athlone

Dutton P. (1989), 'Moving Images? The Parliamentary Recruiting Committee's Poster Campaign', *IWM Review*, Number 4, p43, London, IWM

Eckersley T. (1954), *Poster Design*, London, Studio

Games A. (1960), *Over My Shoulder*, London, Studio

Gentleman D. (1972), *Design in Miniature*, London, SV

Hardie M. & Sabin A.K. (1920), *War Posters*, London, A&C Black

Joyce P. (2003), *The Rule of Liberty*, London, Verso

Lovell A. & Hillier J. (1972), *Studies in Documentary*, London, S&W (Cinema One)

Lucas E.V. (1924), *The Pageant of Empire*, London, LNER

Mackenzie J. (2001), *The Victorian Vision*, London, V&AM

NGS (2003), *Havinden – Advertising and the Artist*, Edinburgh, NGS

Newsinger J. (1999), *Orwell's Politics*, Basingstoke, Palgrave

Orna B. (1967), 'Growing Scope for Stamp Design', *Penrose Annual*, Volume 60, p143, London, Lund Humphries

Perry C.R. (1992), *The Victorian Post Office*, Woodbridge, RHS

Poovey M. (1995), *Making a Social Body*, Chicago, CUP

Reed H. (1934), *Unit One*, London, Cassell

Rose S. (1980), *Royal Mail Stamps*, London, Phaidon

Saler M.T. (1999), *The Avant Garde in Interwar Britain*, Oxford, OUP

Schaffer S. (1994), 'Babbage's Intelligence

Calculating Engines and the Factory System', *Critical Inquiry*, Volume 21, Number 1, p203, Chicago, UCP

Schleger P. (2001), *Hans Schleger – A Life in Design*, London, LH

Spufford S. & Uglow J. (1996), *Cultural Babbage*, London, Faber

Tallents S. (1955), *The Projection of England*, London, Olen Press and Film Centre Ltd (first published in 1932 by Faber)

THE BRITISH
POSTAL
MUSEUM
&ARCHIVE

Our history through the post

Founded in 2004, The British Postal Museum and Archive (BPMA) is the leading resource for all aspects of British postal history. It cares for the visual, physical and written records of over 400 years of postal heritage. This includes material spanning all aspects of GPO design – from stamp and poster artwork, to photographs, pillar boxes and vehicles, along with the business records that provide the historical background to their design and development. The BPMA is custodian of two significant collections: the Royal Mail Archive and the museum collection of the former National Postal Museum. Records in the Royal Mail Archive are designated as being of outstanding national importance.

For further information visit www.postalheritage.org.uk

A Postman in the Blitz (Keeping Calm and Carrying On)
London, 1940

The Postie and WWII
The Post Office played a crucial part in WWII. The great human
displacements associated with military action, evacuation and
production provided a context in which communication and morale
were closely associated. The safe passage of mail and the continuity
of service provided by the Post Office gave a powerful sense of
reassurance and normality to the wider population.